W9-BYB-746

Bebe's **B** Book

El libro **B** de Bebé

WRITTEN BY **J. L. MAZZEO**
ILLUSTRATED BY **HELEN ROSS REVUTSKY**

dingles&company New Jersey

First Printing

Published By dingles&company
P.O. Box 508
Sea Girt, New Jersey 08750

LIBRARY OF CONGRESS CATALOG CARD NUMBER
2005928360

ISBN
ISBN-13 978-1-59646-425-4
ISBN-10 1-59646-425-9

Printed in the United States of America

My Letter Library series is based on the original concept of Judy Mazzeo Zocchi.

ART DIRECTION
Barbie Lambert & Rizco Design
DESIGN
Rizco Design
ENGLISH EDITED BY
Andrea Curley
SPANISH EDITED BY
Jerina Page
PROJECT MANAGER
Lisa Aldorasi
EDUCATIONAL CONSULTANT
Maura Ruane McKenna
PRE-PRESS BY
Pixel Graphics

EXPLORE THE LETTERS OF THE ALPHABET WITH MY LETTER LIBRARY*

Aimee's **A** Book
Bebe's **B** Book
Cassie's **C** Book
Delia's **D** Book
Emma's **E** Book
Faye's **F** Book
George's **G** Book
Henry's **H** Book
Izzy's **I** Book
Jade's **J** Book
Kelsey's **K** Book
Logan's **L** Book
Mia's **M** Book
Nate's **N** Book
Owen's **O** Book
Peter's **P** Book
Quinn's **Q** Book
Rosie's **R** Book
Sofie's **S** Book
Tad's **T** Book
Uri's **U** Book
Vera's **V** Book
Will's **W** Book
Xavia's **X** Book
Yola's **Y** Book
Zach's **Z** Book

* All titles also available in bilingual English/Spanish versions.

WEBSITE
www.dingles.com
E-MAIL
info@dingles.com

My **Letter** Library

Bb

My Letter Library leads young children through the alphabet one letter at a time. By focusing on an individual letter in each book, the series allows youngsters to identify and absorb the concept of each letter thoroughly before being introduced to the next. In addition, it invites them to look around and discover where objects beginning with the specific letter appear in their own world.

Bb

A a **B b** C c D d E e F f G g

H h I i J j K k L l M m N n

O o P p Q q R r S s T t U u

V v W w X x Y y Z z

B is for **B**ebe.

Bebe is a **b**rown **b**ear.

B es para **B**ebé.

Bebé es una osa café.

In Bebe's bedroom
you will find a **b**oat,

En el cuarto de Bebé,
encontrarás un **b**ote,

Bb

bunny slippers
to keep her feet warm,

pantuflas de conejitos para
mantener calientes sus pies

B b

and a blue **b**alloon
from the fair.

y un globo azul
que trajo de la feria.

Bb

By Bebe's bouncy bed
you will find
butterscotch candy,

Cerca de la cama
brincadora de Bebé,
encontrarás dulces
de mantequilla,

Bb

a **b**lock for learning letters,

un cubo para

aprender las letras

Bb

and a beautiful **b**utterfly
that flew in through
the window.

y una bella mariposa
que entró por la ventana.

Bb

On Bebe's floor
you will find a **b**anana
to slice for breakfast,

En el piso de Bebé,
encontrarás un plátano
para rebanar y comer
en el desayuno,

Bb

a **b**utton from
her favorite sweater,

un **b**otón de
su suéter favorito

Bb

and a **b**each **b**all

she bought on vacation.

y una pelota de playa que

compró en sus vacaciones.

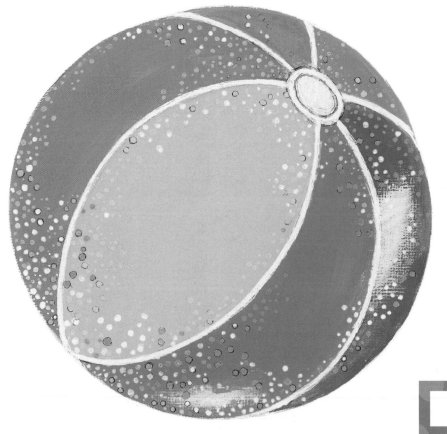

Bb

Things that begin with
the letter **B** are all around.

Cosas que empiezan
con la letra **B** están
por todas partes.

BOAT
BOTE

BUNNY SLIPPERS
PANTUFLAS DE CONEJITOS

BALLOON
GLOBO

BUTTERSCOTCH CANDY
DULCES DE MANTEQUILLA

BLOCK
CUBO

BUTTERFLY
MARIPOSA

BANANA
PLÁTANO

BUTTON
BOTÓN

BEACH **B**ALL
PELOTA DE PLAYA

Where in Bebe's bedroom can they be found?

¿En dónde las puedes encontrar en el cuarto de Bebé?

Have a **"B"** Day!

Read "B" stories all day long.
Read books about bears, bunnies, boats, butterflies, and other **B** words. Then have the child pick out all of the words and pictures starting with the letter **B**.

Make a "B" Craft: A Butterfly
Trace a large butterfly shape on a 12-x-18-inch piece of construction paper. Then have the child cut out the traced butterfly.

Next, he or she should tear pieces of multicolored construction paper into small pieces.

Glue the small pieces of construction paper on the butterfly's wings.

Let the glue dry and enjoy the **"B"** butterfly!

Make a "B" Snack: Chocolate-Covered Bananas
- Peel a ripe banana.
- Insert a Popsicle stick through one end of the banana.
- Melt regular milk chocolate in a saucepan.
- Dip the banana in the melted chocolate.
- Refrigerate and enjoy!

For additional **"B"** Day ideas and a reading list, go to www.dingles.com.

About **Letters**

Use the My Letter Library series to teach a child to identify letters and recognize the sounds they make by hearing them used and repeated in each story.

Ask:
- What letter is this book about?
- Can you name all of the **B** pictures on each page?
- Which **B** picture is your favorite? Why?
- Can you find all of the words in this book that begin with the letter **B**?

ENVIRONMENT
Discuss objects that begin with the letter **B** in the child's immediate surroundings and environment.

Use these questions to further the conversation:
- What is your bedroom like?
- Do you share a bedroom? If so, with whom?
- Do you have a favorite bear or bunny? What is its name?
- Do you have a favorite food that begins with the letter **B**? What is It?

OBSERVATIONS
The My Letter Library series can be used to enhance the child's imagination. Encourage the child to look around and tell you what he or she sees.

Ask:
- Do you have a pretend telephone like Bebe has?
- If you do, whom do you pretend to call?
- What is your favorite **B** object at home? Why?
- Where do bunnies live?
- Where do bears live?

TRY SOMETHING NEW...
Plant a garden with a parent and see how many butterflies it attracts.

J. L. MAZZEO grew up in Middletown, New Jersey, as part of a close-knit Italian American family. She currently resides in Monmouth County, New Jersey, and still remains close to family members in heart and home.

HELEN ROSS REVUTSKY was born in St. Petersburg, Russia, where she received a degree in stage artistry/ design. She worked as the directing artist in Kiev's famous Governmental Puppet Theatre. Her first book, *I Can Read the Alphabet,* was published in Moscow in 1998. Helen now lives in London, where she has illustrated several children's books.